ADVANCE PRAISE FOR *THE INVISIБ*

"Ellen Hinsey's mind bears witness to an unprecedented ability to never abandon poetry, even when approaching the extreme limits of the darkness of our time. In this *Invisible Fugue*, following step by step the movement of Beethoven's *Große Fuge* Op.133, her poetry ventures into a new, ecstatic dimension, where, 'released from the black chaos of the unmanifest,' the earth appears as if in the splendor of the first day, beyond all possible destruction."

 —Giorgio Agamben, author of *Hölderlin's Madness. Chronicle of a Dwelling Life*

"There's an omniscient beauty and wisdom in the intrepid music Ellen Hinsey distills from natural wonder, from spiritual anguish and bewilderment. With roots in Beethoven's most radical, futuristic composition, the *Große Fuge*, Hinsey's *The Invisible Fugue* (presented on the page like a score!) compels as both existential quest and far-reaching cosmic aria. After her previous volume, *The Illegal Age*, which confronted the chilling unraveling of democracy in our imperiled era, these new 'mystical lyrics' (a decade in the making) arrive as a gust of splendid lyricism—a metaphysical thunder shower. The timeless poise and elegance of Hinsey's profound and sibylline project, enhanced by her masterly command of cadence and lineation—artfully crafted in the face of carnage, fear, spiritual outcry, and earthly chaos—is unmatched by any other English language poet writing today."

 —Cyrus Cassells, author of *The World That the Shooter Left Us*

"If a fugue is something you hear, what is *The Invisible Fugue* of Ellen Hinsey's? It is a sourceless source, and this mystery—an 'unlikely coming into being'—is what animates the lyrics of this collection. I've read Hinsey's work for years, and every time the language and form feel constitutional, something upon which to be made, or unmade. *The Invisible Fugue* is no different: Hinsey looks for 'the fixed point of the unexpected' and manages to hold a tone both urgent and unhurried; fugitive and full of feeling; filled with knowing and filled beyond knowing."

 —Pádraig Ó Tuama, host of *Poetry Unbound* from On Being Studios

"Ellen Hinsey's poetry balances between a deep engagement with the socio-political world and a rich inner realm. This collection stands out for its distinct mysticism—yet remains non-religious—characterized by its restrained poetic diction, minimalism, and musical elegance. It's a stylized, empathetic lyricism of artful gesture, reminiscent of Buddhist koans and German mystics, echoing the 'psalms of. . .creation.' A masterful fugue of the *via negativa*."

   —Jarosław Płuciennik, author of *The Courage of Poetics*

"A fugue, etymologically rendered, is flight. There might well have been a flight in Ellen Hinsey's *The Invisible Fugue*—a fleeing from the hammer blows of time—but she is finally too honest a poet for that. I don't mean to deny her long and patient attention to the unnatural solvents of love and the uncertain prospects of a reckoning. I simply note the uniqueness of this revelatory volume, written in the wildly inventive (because impossible) idiom of mystical lyrics. The song of praise there is no leap of faith; it is 'unwilled devotion' to a generosity that defies finality of vision. This is spirituality for a heart-breaking age."

   —James Wetzel, author of *Parting Knowledge*

THE INVISIBLE FUGUE

ELLEN HINSEY

THE INVISIBLE FUGUE

Wildhouse Poetry

Published by Wildhouse Poetry, an imprint of Wildhouse Publishing (wildhousepublishing.com). No part of this book may be reproduced in any manner without the written permission of the publisher, except in brief quotations embodied in critical articles or reviews. Contact info@wildhousepublications.com.

Front panel "The Inspiration of Saint Matthew" (detail) by Caravaggio, reproduced by permission of Scala Archives.

With grateful acknowledgment to Bärenreiter-Verlag for their permission to reproduce the opening of Beethoven's works, Opus 133 and Opus 130.

Printed in the USA

ISBN: 978-1-961741-08-9

Illegible this world
PAUL CELAN

CONTENTS

THE INVISIBLE FUGUE

Opus 133

Dann hör ich oft die Stimme des Donnerers
Am Mittag, wenn der eherne nahe kommt

It's then I often hear the thunderer's voice
At noon, when he brazenly comes near

Friedrich Hölderlin

I

1.

"Wrapped in the shadows of eternal solitude,
in the impenetrable darkness of the thicket,
impenetrable, immeasurable, unapproachable,
formlessly extended—"

(Diary, No. 312, 1823)

I.
Overtura. Allegro

Tonight, under this thunderous sky—you are called
                  In midnight's last hour—to witness how

The splendor of that First Season was wrested
                  From tempest of void and roiling vapor—

Released from the black chaos of the unmanifest—

This unlikely *coming into being*—watched over
                    By Enigmatic sight—secreted means: *you*

Who know this hour, and through your drive,
                    Fashioned its unfathomable intent: igniting

Space with life's downward thrust, imperishable—

Tonight—walking out under this unfinished sky—
 In the solitary hour of pitch dark, black-splashed

Shadows mooring across the fields—the forest
 Engulfed: the cypress's restless

 Flame uprising:

*Alone under this illuminated sky—*under your wide

Invention—*in its ever-wider singing, yet turning*
Back towards source: time's compass unstrung—

Released from linearity—with First Principles
Surpassing understanding: *Tonight, beneath this sky,*

With fragmented consciousness, *I try again*

To grasp some scale of understanding—as now, knee deep
                         In damp field, I stand stilled—witness to how

Your great fire still surges, this ever-burning map:
                         The trailing rotation of the massing
                                       Planetary realms—

In their constant pitch of spheres, circulating stars—

The eye's gaze—*straining to seize how light still*
                         Pierces your vast habitat—the prison of distance—

Tunnelling time-burdened towards an outstretched palm—
                         Waiting at night amid a field, earth's rust at ankle—

Circled by all creation that lives in pleated undergrowth

And mud: *the snail's involute shell—armored insects,*
In-folded wing of crow: all bent to silence in your night

Room: where the scent of once sun-stunned fields
Rises to perfume the black—
And where we, fixed, remain—

Mind trying to rise to such splendor, but instead—

Embroiled in our world of shadow intent: *for even*
                    In love's sphere, holding the beloved under your sheltering

Absence, the heart persists in waywardness and loss:
                    Possessed by time, the decree of seasons, restless
                                        Impulse—

All merciless archers, ruthlessly stalking us, even here—

In the dark. You: Great Architect of the Imperial Realm—

                  Eternal refuge, power of witness and enduring psalm—

Now—*by dusk-engulfed scrub, knotted vine, old ravine*—

                Though attentive I wait—

                        Still, your calm breaks at a far

Distance from my rooted form: *in light-raging night.*

II

2.

"What you are, you are by accident of birth—"

(Diary, No. 180, 1822)

"And when we arrive, oppressed
By time, uncertainty's weight—"

(Notebook, No. 1)

II.
Meno, Mosso e Moderato

In midnight's sanctuary: *we are left to wonder*—
How, like all once *unmade*, we too have fallen

Into being: entrusted to the temporal world,
Under enigmatic skies, surveying stony terrain—

This *coming into being*, like crossing the infinitesimal line—

That separates gray dawn-water from watery sky—
And driven into time—we wade forward alone—

With only fragmentary instincts, propelled downstream
Into the wake of *the unpredictable human tide—*

*Where, at the unforeseen hour—*voyaging the edge

Of road-black, we ask: this tentative arrival for which
                              There is no map, only an *enduring in complexity*—

The always imperfect hour of birth—issued from
                              That First Grammar we can never learn—
                                                      But which is

Repeated nightly in the cryptic lament of ripening fields:

To not understand being—but emerge from its great

                        Declensions of cases—*First vowels and First tense*—

Of which we are always, and ever, mere fragment:

                        Sharing with all creation that ancient script:

                                                  present

In the archaic imperative of the pine's vertical thrust—

The elliptical language of hoarfrost—glimpsed in
                    The gale's litany in weeds: *their wild veer and list*—

All in-patterns of the cosmos' intent: *all written*
                    With us into embedded darkness—
                                        All inscribed

With mystery of purpose—but ripe with possibility:

Against which we try our unstable logic: *thrusting us*
Ever deeper into the Mind's impenetrable thicket—

As if we were not, like all things: raised from cells
Sunken in ravine-damp or desert clay, from

Which generation flares, *and from which we also emerge—*

Beside all that briefly blooms, then returns to decay—
                          (Threatened by the hand's bloodforce and doubt—)

For on what to base this arrival into the world—
                          On what the framing of act: what meaning
                                              Trespassing

Into day—arising on a horizon of ash and amber:

Filled only with vague hope and unreliable will—
                    And the desire to be stilled—*in the fragilely grasped hour*

Of insight—that retreats as we advance: *Enigmatic*
                    Trajectory—which prods, then refuses: leaving us standing

Alone at night in damp fields—awaiting early shadow.

III

3.

"In my solitude here—"

(Diary, No. 194, 1811)

III.
Allegro

———————

If from midnight's darkness—we go forth in first daylight,
　　　　　　　Among all that is manifest—among the myriad wealth

Of the unending earth: the road bathed in gray cast,
　　　　　　　Above which the sun's path
　　　　　　　　　　　　Begins its singular passage—

If unarmed with anything other than sight—

We advance: discovering wild grass full of dew-caught
                        Sense—*reeds still bearing the asymmetrical traces*

Of their night-capture: bent branch and thorn-bramble,
                     All scripts from the mysterious
                                 Gesture of the unseen—

If we go forth along roadside—fields rough-ploughed,

Shadowed: still sheltering the secretive fox, anxious
                              Field mouse—*and all other fragile, tentative beings*

That inhabit the realms of your always renewing fields—
                            In their seasons of bloom and retreat:
                                              Stark in snow,

But complete when wheat's chevron rises, heat-struck—

If we advance along roadway—beside a city's approaching ruin—
　　　　　　　　Witnessing the silence of abandoned lots,

Above which inland gulls in their scavenging circles turn—
　　　　　　　　Dive to debris—*and blot out the early*

　　　　　　　　　　　　　　　　　Rising

Light—but also signal the levity of airborne things, *if*—

We advance slowly—uncertain: fearful of direction—
                But full in that hour of the fragile hope of encounter:

To not just discover tight fronds among weeds—
                Or the paper-white of innocent birch—
                                But the unique,

Beloved *other*—the one for whom we are made—

Who, in their own going-forth, hard-earned breath—
                Also arises in hesitant wakefulness, also wades into

Day's unfolding—shouldering the weight of doubt—
                The impress of grief, *if unknowingly,*
                              We go forth—

Under the same wide expanse of sky—searching for

The exact coordinates: fixed point of the *unexpected* —
　　　　　　Where, even before *arrival*, as if anticipated—*as if*—

Signaled from afar: something *familiar* in the unfamiliar
　　　　　　Approaches, *and there arises the hope*
　　　　　　　　　　Of shared covenant—

And home. A desire earned from all the pilgrim hours,

Solitary steps, and steadfast carrying on: this *other*—
                  Present now on midday's path, who nears—finds us,

Beauty uncontained in feature, but alive in gesture:
                  There—at the unmarked turn when we reach
                                  Arrival—

Then, under the sky's dome: *it seems day has bestowed*

On us momentary release, which trumps black solitude
                    And the stationary heart: *though it is with fear we near*

This crux in time, *where the tempo of endurance slows—*
                    And the air, as if before storm,
                                        Opens to the unforeseen—

For loss still lies in each step—*and day's ever-changeable*

Storms can undo bright harvest—even as high summer
> Rises and reigns above: *and backwards towards earth*

All loving goes—still in this hour, now, this desired:
> To reach this *other* of your creatures—
>> With whom

We seek shelter—for these unsheltered hours on earth.

IV

4.

"To you only do I confide this as a secret—"

(Diary, No. 194, 1800)

"To join with the rage,
The fire of time—"

(Notebook, No. 2)

IV.
Allegro Molto e Con Brio

—————————————————

—————————————————

Meridiem. The sun stationed overhead: a beacon turned scythe—
                    Sharpening light's shaft of borne-down blaze,

Seeking swift execution of the harvest's near-fullness,
                    Of wasteland weeds—or valley
                                        Of burgeoning grain—

All edged by the enduring kingdom of river quarry:

—————————————————

But for now—*all still unfolding, minute by minute*—
                    Under the wide eye of noon's apex—
                                        Where, kept from

The great flow and flux (which advances in each
                    Second): in this moment—
                                        After the unlikely encounter —

With skin alive—*under the azure fire of the illuminated*

World—wishing to be part of its ecstatic nature, *then*—

                                    When we are finally held

Fast by the gaze that renders intelligible our

                    Catalogue of eclipsed nights—

                                    Sharing flesh's proximity

We hunger towards the threshold *of desire's release*—

Where to touch you, other—under the temporary shelter
                        Of a roof—*behind a shade's false crepuscule*—

Woven together on a becalmed sea of a white bed,
                        We invite it all: trespass into this world—
                                                Wrestle

Under the light—embrace now—*with wild pulse:*

To finally let you, *other*, near—let noon's tide of heat

                      Bring us toward *the ancient covenant of*

                                    Hand on breast—

The arabesque exhange of caress, skin's empire of sweat—

                      Where touch's divining discovers:

                                    Cherished curve

Of flank—coveted inlet of neck: *the back's taut*

Tension—the male torso with its suspension, *action*—
        Love spreading—like a beneficent tributary
                Over the dry

Scoured land, releasing day's captivity: making one
        Of our separateness, in embrace,
              Desire and need,

Loss and bewilderment—until I hear you—*other,*

Rustically rejoice, *fall back into breath*—spent, full,
Of our shared harvest of *emptiness*.
Then—when

Our helix breaks back into its exile-filled parts—
And we silently lie together, where
Bright loss returns—

Finding us hiding in innocence, in afternoon's dusk—

Where shadows threaten roadside: night advancing

                         Toward us with its pendulous step and sure—*redrawing*

Limits, the unlikely moment of our union ended—

                    Flesh separating back into its specificity—

                                               Dragging

Comprehension in its wake: *the dark watchfully*

Descending—the Word refusing and refused: *love's*
                           Holy alphabet falling mute. Then—when stillness

Returns to where we have stationed our hearts—
                           Under noon's archer sun—*and the*
                                          planetary night—

We find our road razed *by desire's rage*—and fire.

V

5.

"My dominion is in the air...into tones
That sound, and roar and storm—"

(Diary, No. 31, 1814)

"How is it...to not be permitted
To love the earth forever, undone by the
Storms of time—"

(Notebook, No. 3)

V.
Fuga

———————————

Abandoned to this wild rushing: with its insistent

                     Onward rage: punctuated by *the sudden breaking*

Of day, then cover—all consumed in variation

                     And flight: into which we descend, *try to hold fast—*

To the cliff's steep incline—*vertiginous pine, the narrative*

Of fallow and full, then—*onward*, speed a decree—
                    A verdict, while we—*never suspended,*
                                        Never released—

Thrown towards the fire of hours: a bent branch
                    With wind constantly on us—
                                        Unanchored, but persisting

Thrust forward under cloudcover—beside the fall

Of decaying cities: caught up in uncertainty's
                      Marled branches—*morning, afternoon, evening*—

Consumed: *onward*—threshed like earth's old quarries
                     Of granite, sand, salt—abrupt storms
                                 In-breaking with their

Blizzard of forces: *like the gale that pulls us under*—

Like grief that carves out our sleepless hours: calamity,
That fierce decree of weather—*the approaching*
Undercut

Of loss arriving like the banked-up construction
Of the cloud's imperial thunderhead:
All air-forged hail,

Downward pummel, the scouring rain—*pain lashing*

Us like exposed marshland reeds: force of tempest—

                Then, intermittent: light's balm returning—*itinerant,*

Wandering shadows coming again over the fields—

                Beneficent, simple, without calculation,

                                Or aim—*no*

Anchor or intent—just the endless *going on*—

The battered stubble of harvested fields—black battalions
                              Of beetles, rain-ravaged stalks—*abandoned grapes,*

The earth's cicatrices: stumps, matted furrows, washed-out
                              Gullies—*then return*:
                                                            All the miraculous reversals

From ruin: *the purple belled flower behind barbed wire*—

The lichen-tattooed vine stump preparing for spring:
        Sweetness, earth wells—*onward*: Time, the eternal ruler

With its brutal scale of tenses—*gestation, maturity, decay*—
        The body drifting, the aging hand,
                The limbs stiffening—

Each day: discontent, restlessness, spite, *respite*—

Waiting, anxiety, willfulness, simplicity—rage:
> Against its mass and master, who nevertheless drives

The pack on: *the dusk's knife-precision limning*
> *Vine and root*—its etched cross-hatching—
>> *Shading day*

Back into blackness, the terrain renouncing its palette:

Green to grey earth—*the gorge dark-swallowing its*
                    Tributary, until the smoky last hour of birdcall:

When the white moth rises, falls, one last time among
                    The rocks—for there is no respite:
                                        Only horizon, air

And touch—*against the supremacy of the Emperor hours.*

VI

6.

".. is immaterial, and for this reason
transcends every conception. [...] But from
what we observe is eternal, omnipotent,
omniscient and omnipresent—

(Diary, No. 322, 1816)

"And on that day
When different *and* same
Were one, and all reached into
The thunderous silence—"

(Notebook, No. 4)

VI.
Allegro

These solitary hours on earth—each instant hunted
                    By imperfection: *arrival—but then loss of direction,*

To not fathom the design that draws us—issued
                    From unlanguageable complexity:
                                        These exiled hours—

Removed from that silence that sounds us   _____
                    Through

All creation—as we labor across the unfinished earth—
                    Where there is no advance—*only endless*
                                        Carrying on—

While we: stung by deep desire—are undone by *want*—
                    Where only *Center* sustains, but eludes:
                                        Erratic

Target of the heart: torn between animal—and

                    _____

                    Illumination—

Where our brief verticality: allotted breath, our pulse—
                    Beating out the tone-length of our approaching
                                                    Abandon—

Yet when—in the innocent silence of the fields, unbidden—
                    Intimations of that higher realm rise, when—You

Generously reveal your intricate net—threaded

                    ———————
                    Throughout

The indivisible landscape: exposing its secreted matrix—
                    When vision is failed by common sight—becomes

Night—*when You emit that single high frequency of being*—
                    Understructure that eludes interpretation—
                                                      I follow—

Briefly held captive—then, released: *tongue full of*

                    ———————
                    Testimony

Of Your illustrious trace: in that instant when the soul rises
                              In its *all-desire*—for that which it can never reach—

And *You*—interior of telling—lift me into your updraft,
                              Towards that thunderous octave of

                                                            Silence—

(Written in no key) but spring of all that inwardly

                              ———

                              Pulses:

Pulled towards some unsuspected apex in air—where
The good seeks the *Good*, that mystical lodestone—

And returns with the shadow of *Love*—then Your—
Radiance, Illumination, Resilience, Impress,
Presence,

Endurance, Tenacity, Incitement, Ferocity—*Alphabet of*

———————

Insight—

Your all-knowing that roils in the essence of being—
This power: intangibly concrete and untamed—

Not balm: but raging source, bracing as night
Wind that violently thrashes
The fragile spring staves—

All then, suddenly—rendered speechless:

—————

Roughened

With loss of compass, *and incomplete way to say*
                    You, who are without time and *heedless of need—*

You—who, in that rarest hour, once drew close
                    In the silence of the light-blasted field—
                                        Revealing

The force through which I am driven,
                    _____

                    Accompanied

And found: *You*—fierce spirit-mercury of the First Season—
                    Determinant that stubbornly binds—with its bold

Intent: *You*, so singly-arrowed throughout—*You*
                    Will not spare me—though I am voice,
                                        —and compelled

To sing your praises before my night.

VII

Cavatina, Opus 130

7.
*"Sometimes it pleased Thee to let me feel
the heavy hand of Thy displeasure
and to humiliate my proud heart—"*

(Diary, No. 323, 1816)

VII.
Molto expressivo

If with this knowledge, I advance unwillingly towards
                        Your night, it is because I have feasted on the psalms

Of your creation: *you have made a path for me through*
                    The vineyard—with its spare notes
                                    Of ripening grapes,

Whose tendrils reach towards your sun: each filled

With the perfect music of unfolding: *if I wish to remain*
Among your sun-parched fields—where lizards hide

In the dried, fissured walls and ivy binds day and brick
Together: if I love the black plum,
The balm of distance—

If praise is still the resolute verdict of my tongue—

In your Kingdom—*if I wish the path to extend a bit*
                              Further: if I wish to walk again down to your green

Pastures: where the stream ignites its liquid music,
                              And the uprising trees craze the sky—
                                                            When summer

Is high, and reigns above: *if I wish to walk out under*

Your great vault—under night's duress of damp—

                Where the planetary realm recounts its ancient tale

Of passage: *if the Great Wakefulness that is yours draws*

                Me forth—with unwilled devotion to

                        Your generosity,

Which holds all accounts in store—with a logic that

Is incalculable—*but written into each helix and leaf,*
Into each cell's tight matrix—it is because at Time's

Crossroads I have felt your encrypted presence—
Have seen oneness surge from beneath
Appearances,

And bind the Whole into your bright net, knotted

With complexity—pulsing with your conception that
              Is ageless, indeterminate undercurrent, but awake

In all creation—*if I know that above and below*—in
                    The silence and the mystery,
                                        Your presence drives me—

If the foot's journey is arduous—*yet prods us*

To go on with purpose: the road roughly sewn

                With dried weed, rot, wind-decay of the common

Flower—*if loss indeed carves out day's details*—

              If I, sound-blasted by the single

                          Note of *being*,

Know that you are also the bringer of that night

Which is nightless, but filled with your hammer—
And, in the end, all is blessed—spent, beneath its

Silent blows—I know no hour when I have not
Been mastered by its force: that First—
Last power—

Testified, watched over,
By Time's restless fury and chariot.

NOTES

NOTES

Epigraph, page vii: "Der blinde Sänger" (The Blind Singer) by Friedrich Hölderlin.

OVERTURA / ALLEGRO

(1.) Diary (No. 312): "Wrapped in the shadows of eternal solitude..." *Beethoven: The Man and the Artist, as Revealed in his own Words* (New York: B.W. Hubsch, 1905).

MENO, MOSSO ET MODERATO

(2.) Diary (No. 180): "What you are you are by accident of birth...", *Beethoven: The Man and the Artist.*

Notebook (No. 1): "And when we arrive, oppressed by time, uncertainty's weight..." (author's notebooks).

ALLEGRO

(3.) Diary (No. 194): "In my solitude here..." *Beethoven: The Man and the Artist.*

ALLEGRO MOLTO E CON BRIO

(4.) Diary (No. 194): "To you only do I confide this as a secret..." *Beethoven: The Man and the Artist.*

Notebook (No. 2): "To join with the rage, the fire of time..." (author's notebooks).

FUGA

(5.) Diary (No. 31): "My dominion is in the air…" *Beethoven: The Man and the Artist.*

Notebook (No. 3): "How is it…to not be permitted to love the earth forever, undone by the storms of time…" (author's notebooks).

ALLEGRO

(6.) Diary (No. 322): "…is immaterial, and for this reason, transcends every conception…" *Beethoven: The Man and the Artist.*

Notebook (No. 4): "And on that day when *different* and *same* were one, and all reached into the thunderous silence…" (author's notebooks).

Fugue VI is dedicated to Dwight R. Walsh, whose wisdom guides me each day. *καὶ ἡ εἰρήνη τοῦ θεοῦ ἡ ὑπερέχουσα πάντα νοῦν.*

MOLTO EXPRESSIVO

(7.) Diary (No. 323): "Sometimes it pleased Thee to let me feel the heavy hand of Thy displeasure…" *Beethoven: The Man and the Artist.*

Musical notation: The *Cavatina* is from Beethoven's String Quartet No. 13, Op. 130, for which the *Große Fuge* was originally written.

*

The Invisible Fugue *was composed over a decade, beginning in August 2013. While this poetic sequence was originally conceived independently from Beethoven's* Große Fuge, Op. 133, *this work at times accompanied the poem through its unfolding. Among other texts, the Upanishads—allusions to which appear in Beethoven's notebooks—have also long served as inspiration. Readers may observe that certain sections of the poem are written in "keys" of letters such as S, F and I, among others. I would like to express my gratitude to those individuals who provided support while this book was being written: A. and M. who kept the manuscript safe under uncertain conditions; Marlyse et Daniel Delay, deux esprits extraordinaires, qui ont ouvert leur maison et m'ont offert la majestie de leur amitié; and Dr. Neil Forsyth for his precious friendship and "the upper room," without which* The Invisible Fugue *would not have been written.*

———————

Ellen Hinsey is the author of nine books of poetry, essays, dialogue and literary translation. Her most recent volume of poetry, *The Illegal Age*, explores the rise of authoritarianism and was a National Poetry Series Finalist and the Poetry Book Society's 2018 Autumn Choice. Hinsey's first-hand reports and essays on dangers to democracy are collected in *Mastering the Past: Contemporary Central and Eastern Europe and the Rise of Illiberalism*. Her other volumes of poetry include *Update on the Descent*, also a National Poetry Series Finalist, which draws on her experience at the International Criminal Tribunal for the former Yugoslavia in The Hague, *The White Fire of Time*, and *Cities of Memory*, which received the Yale Younger Poets Award. Hinsey's book-length dialogue with the Lithuanian poet Tomas Venclova, *Magnetic North*, was a finalist for Lithuania's Book of the Year and has appeared in seven languages. She is the recipient of numerous awards and her work has appeared in many publications, including *The New York Times*, *The New Yorker*, *The Irish Times*, *Poetry*, *Poetry Review*, *The Paris Review*, *Der Tagesspiegel*, and others. A former Berlin Prize fellow of the American Academy in Berlin, she taught for many years at Skidmore College in Paris and has most recently been a visiting professor at Georg-August-Universität Göttingen, Germany. Hinsey is the international correspondent for *The New England Review*.

Printed in the USA
CPSIA information can be obtained
at www.ICGtesting.com
LVHW061731111223
766214LV00013B/298